JINGLE CASH

Jingle Cash

Sabastian Tonis

CONTENTS

1

CHAPTER 1: JINGLE ALL THE WAY TO EXTRA CASH

WHY THE HOLIDAYS ARE THE PERFECT TIME TO HUSTLE

The holidays are a magical time filled with twinkling lights, festive music, and the aroma of freshly baked cookies wafting through the air. But let's be real: they can also be a financial tightrope walk. That's why this season is the perfect opportunity to roll up your sleeves and dive into some holiday hustles. From crafting unique ornaments to baking scrumptious treats, there are endless ways to make some extra cash while spreading cheer. Who knew that holiday spirit could also boost your wallet?

First up on the hustle list is seasonal craft selling. Whether you're a whiz at knitting cozy scarves or have a knack for making snazzy ornaments, this is your time to shine! Set up a booth at local craft fairs or even sell your creations online through platforms like Etsy. Not only will you get to showcase your creativity, but you'll also be making money doing something you love. Plus, who wouldn't want to deck the halls with handmade decorations? It's a win-win!

Then there's online tutoring during the holiday break. Students often have a little extra time off, and many parents are looking for ways to keep their kids engaged and learning. If you have a skill to share, whether it's math, reading, or even a foreign language, you can offer your services online. Create a fun and engaging tutoring experience that makes learning feel like a holiday gift instead of a chore. Trust us, those little ones will appreciate the extra help, and you'll appreciate the extra cash!

If you're looking for a hustle that's all about spreading cheer, consider freelance gift wrapping. Everyone loves beautifully wrapped presents, but not everyone has the time or skill to do it themselves. Offer your wrapping services to busy friends, family, and neighbors. You can even set up a wrapping station at local markets or events. With some festive music playing and your creative flair, you'll turn ordinary gifts into extraordinary treasures, all while earning some jingle in your pocket.

Lastly, let's not forget about the delicious world of baking and catering! The holidays are synonymous with sweet treats and hearty meals, making it the perfect time to whip up some goodies to sell. Whether it's cookies, cakes, or even festive catering, your kitchen can become a bustling hub of holiday cheer. Don't overlook the opportunity to rent out holiday equipment and décor either. From inflatable snowmen to twinkling lights, many families are looking to create that perfect holiday atmosphere without the hassle of storing decorations year-round. So, gather your family, brainstorm some fun ideas, and let the holiday hustling begin!

SETTING REALISTIC GOALS FOR YOUR HOLIDAY HUSTLE

Setting realistic goals for your holiday hustle is like crafting the perfect gingerbread house: you need a solid foundation, some sweet decorations, and a sprinkle of creativity. First things first, let's take a moment to dream big! Picture yourself raking in some extra cash to buy that special gift for your loved ones or treating the family to a festive outing. But before you start imagining stacks of cash, let's ground those dreams with achievable goals that will keep your holiday hustle fun and stress-free.

Start by breaking down your overall goal into bite-sized pieces. If you want to earn $500 by Christmas, that might sound daunting at first. But if you divide it into weekly targets, it becomes much more manageable! For instance, aiming to make $100 each week through your chosen hustle could mean selling handmade ornaments, offering online tutoring sessions, or wrapping gifts for neighbors. This approach not only makes your goals clearer but also allows you to celebrate small wins along the way—like finally mastering that perfect cookie recipe for your holiday baking side gig!

Next, consider the resources you already have at your disposal. Do you have a stash of craft supplies waiting to be transformed into stunning holiday decorations? Or perhaps you're a whiz at math and can share that knowledge through online tutoring during the school break? Assessing your strengths and available materials will help you choose a hustle that aligns with your skills and makes the most of what you already own. This way, you won't just be hustling harder; you'll be hustling smarter, leaving more time for family festivities.

Time management is another key ingredient in your holiday hustle recipe. The holiday season can become a whirlwind of activities, from decorating the tree to baking cookies for school parties. It's crucial to carve out specific time slots for your hustle amidst the holiday chaos. Whether it's dedicating a couple of hours on weekends for Christmas light installation or setting aside an evening for gift wrapping, creating a schedule will help you stay on track without feeling overwhelmed. Plus, you'll have more time to enjoy those cozy family moments that make the season so special.

Lastly, remember to keep it fun! The holiday hustle should bring joy, not stress. Involve the kids in your projects, whether it's crafting decorations or baking holiday treats. This not only helps them learn valuable skills but also strengthens family bonds. Celebrate your progress together, whether it's a mini dance party to celebrate a completed order or a cozy movie night after a successful week. By setting realistic goals and keeping the spirit of the season alive, you'll turn your holiday hustle into an exciting adventure that everyone can enjoy!

2

CHAPTER 2: CRAFTY CASH: SEASONAL CRAFT SELLING

Fun and Festive Craft Ideas

Crafting during the holidays is not just a fun way to spend time with your family; it's also a fantastic opportunity to make some extra cash! With a sprinkle of creativity and a dash of holiday spirit, you can turn your craft projects into a money-making venture. Think about making festive ornaments, adorable holiday cards, or even unique decorations that can adorn homes during the holiday season. Gather your kids around the table, pull out the scissors, glue, and glitter, and let the crafting chaos begin! Not only will you create beautiful keepsakes, but you'll also be building skills that could help you earn some jingle for the holidays.

One popular idea is to create handmade decorations. From wreaths made of pinecones to painted mason jars filled with twinkling fairy lights, the possibilities are endless! Kids can get involved by painting, gluing, and assembling, which makes for a great family bonding activity. Once your decorations are ready, consider selling them at local craft fairs or online marketplaces. Don't forget to use social media to showcase your creations; a few well-placed posts can generate interest and attract customers from all around. Plus, who doesn't love a unique, handmade touch during the holidays?

Another fun avenue to explore is baking and catering. The holidays are synonymous with sweet treats and delectable dishes, making this the perfect time to whip up some goodies. Get your kids involved in baking cookies, cakes, or even savory dishes that can be sold to neighbors or at holiday events. Set up a little pop-up shop in your front yard, or offer delivery in your neighborhood. Not only will you fill your home with wonderful scents, but you'll also be able to earn some cash while you do it. Just think about how much fun it would be to create festive holiday treats that everyone will love!

If you have a knack for gift wrapping, don't shy away from offering your services! Many families find the wrapping process tedious and time-consuming, especially during the busy holiday season.

Get your kids on board to help with wrapping gifts in creative and eye-catching ways. You can set up shop in your living room or even offer to wrap gifts for friends and neighbors for a small fee. Add some extra flair with ribbons, bows, and handmade tags to make the gifts stand out. Your clients will appreciate the time saved and the beautiful presentation, and you'll be raking in the holiday cash!

Lastly, consider the booming market for holiday rentals. If you have holiday decorations or equipment like lights, blow-ups, or even a tree you're willing to lend out, you can rent them to families looking to spread some cheer without the hassle of purchasing everything themselves. This is a win-win situation—a neighbor gets to enjoy the festive spirit without spending a fortune, and you get to make some extra cash! So gather your family, brainstorm fun craft ideas, and get ready to turn your holiday creativity into a festive income. With a little effort and imagination, this holiday season can be both joyful and financially rewarding!

Where to Sell Your Crafts: Markets and Online Platforms

When it comes to selling your crafts, the world is your oyster! You can find the perfect spot to showcase your creative talents, whether you prefer the hustle and bustle of local markets or the convenience of online platforms. First up, let's talk about craft fairs and holiday markets. These vibrant gatherings are like treasure troves filled with eager shoppers looking for unique gifts. Set up a booth adorned with your handmade holiday decorations or tasty baked goods, and watch as families flock to your colorful creations. Don't forget to engage with your customers; a friendly smile and a little holiday cheer can go a long way in making a sale!

If you're more of a night owl or just prefer to stay cozy at home, online platforms are a fantastic option. Websites like Etsy and eBay provide a digital storefront where you can list your crafts for a global audience. Snap some eye-catching photos of your handmade items, write enticing descriptions, and set competitive prices. With a little bit of social media magic, you can promote your listings on platforms like Instagram and Facebook, reaching friends and family who might be eager to support your holiday hustle. Plus, the best part? You can work on your shop while wearing your favorite pajamas!

Don't overlook community groups and local social media marketplaces. Facebook Marketplace and neighborhood apps like Nextdoor are great places to connect with people in your area who are on the lookout for special holiday gifts. Post about your crafts, offer local delivery, or even set up a pop-up shop right in your driveway! You'd be surprised at how many neighbors are excited to shop local and support families in their community. This approach not only helps you sell your items but also builds a sense of camaraderie with those around you.

For those who are crafty in different ways, consider diversifying your offerings. If wrapping gifts is your forte, you could start a freelance gift-wrapping service. Everyone loves beautifully wrapped presents, especially during the holiday season! Advertise your skills to busy families who would be thrilled to let someone else handle the wrapping while they focus on holiday celebrations. Similarly, if baking is your passion, think about selling cookies, cakes, or holiday treats to neighbors and friends. Word of mouth can spread like wildfire, especially when it comes to delicious goodies!

Lastly, don't forget about the renting game! If you have holiday decorations or equipment gathering dust in your attic, consider renting them out to families looking to brighten their homes for the season. From Christmas lights to inflatable lawn decorations, there are many folks who would love to borrow festive items without the need to buy them. This can be a win-win situation, providing you with extra cash while helping others create a magical holiday atmosphere. So, whether you're selling crafts at a market, online, or even renting out your festive gear, there are countless ways to make your holiday hustle a success!

Marketing Your Crafts to Holiday Shoppers

When the holiday season rolls around, your crafts can become a magical ticket to extra cash! Imagine transforming your kitchen table into a festive workshop where your creativity dances with the jingle of coins. Whether you're knitting cozy scarves, crafting beautiful ornaments, or baking delicious treats, there's a world of eager holiday shoppers just waiting to discover your unique creations. So, gather your supplies, don your favorite holiday sweater, and let's dive into the jolly journey of marketing your crafts to those festive folks out there!

First things first, let's talk about showcasing your work. Visuals are everything when it comes to catching the eye of holiday shoppers. Make sure to snap bright, cheerful photos of your crafts that scream "pick me!" Use natural light and playful backgrounds—think twinkling lights or a snowy scene—to make your creations pop. If you're selling online, platforms like Etsy or social media can be your best friends. Create an Instagram account filled with mouth-watering pictures of your baked goods or stunning images of your handmade decorations. Remember to use hashtags like #HolidayCrafts and #ShopSmall to attract shoppers who are searching for unique gifts!

Next up, let's spread the word! Word of mouth is a powerful tool, especially during the holidays when everyone is looking for that perfect gift. Don't be shy—tell your family, friends, and neighbors about your crafts. You can even host a holiday open house or pop-up shop where they can come, sip hot cocoa, and browse your creations. If you're feeling extra festive, consider teaming up with other local crafters for a craft fair. This way, you can pool your resources and attract more customers, all while enjoying the holiday spirit together!

Online marketplaces aren't the only way to reach holiday shoppers. Think outside the box! Offer your crafts at local holiday markets or fairs where shoppers flock for unique, handmade gifts. Set up a cheerful booth adorned with holiday decorations, and don't forget to share your story. People love to support local artisans, especially when they know the passion and heart behind each piece. If you're selling baked goods, consider offering samples to entice potential buyers. The smell of fresh cookies or cakes might just lead to a line of eager customers!

Lastly, let's not forget about customer engagement. Once you've made a sale, keep the holiday cheer flowing! Send thank-you notes with a sprinkle of festive magic or a small freebie, like a mini ornament or a cookie sample. Encourage happy customers to leave reviews and share their purchases on social media. Happy customers are your best advertising! By creating a sense of community and joy around your crafts, you'll not only make extra money for the holidays but also spread the warmth of the season—one handmade item at a time. So, grab those crafting supplies and get ready to make this holiday season your most profitable yet!

3

CHAPTER 3: TUTORING WITH TINSEL: ONLINE TUTORING F

Choosing the Right Subjects to Tutor

Choosing the right subjects to tutor can feel like a treasure hunt, especially when you're on the lookout for extra cash during the holiday season. The key is to think about what you enjoy, what you excel at, and what subjects are in high demand. Picture this: you love math, and you're great at it. Why not help a few kids tackle their math homework while you're at it? Not only will you get to share your skills, but you'll also be raking in some extra jingle for those holiday gifts!

Next, consider the subjects that might be a bit more festive. With the holiday spirit in the air, many kids might need a little help in creative subjects like art or writing. If you're a whiz at crafting holiday cards or writing holiday-themed stories, these could be a hit! Families are often on the lookout for ways to keep their little ones engaged, and what better way than to offer a tutoring session filled with creativity and cheer? You'll be the holiday hero, and your bank account will thank you for it!

Don't forget to tap into the tech-savvy side of things. Online tutoring has become all the rage, especially during school breaks. If you're comfortable with technology, consider offering tutoring in subjects like coding, digital art, or even music lessons over video calls. Kids are more likely to sign up for something they can do from the comfort of their homes, and you'll be the one bringing the fun right to their screens. Plus, you can wear your favorite holiday pajamas while you teach—talk about a win-win!

When selecting your tutoring subjects, it's also wise to look around and see what's trending. Are kids buzzing about a new popular book series? Or perhaps there's a new math curriculum they're all tackling? By aligning your subjects with what's hot at the moment, you'll attract more students. You could even craft themed sessions around popular holiday stories, connecting reading with the festivities. This approach not only makes learning enjoyable but also adds a sprinkle of holiday magic to your tutoring sessions.

Lastly, remember that every subject you choose has the potential to add a bit of sparkle to someone's holiday season. Whether you're helping a child understand the basics of algebra or guiding them through a winter-themed art project, your efforts can make a real difference. Choose subjects that excite you, and you'll find that your enthusiasm will shine through, making learning a joyous experience for both you and your students. Happy tutoring, and may your holiday hustle bring you all the cheer (and cash) you desire!

Setting Up Your Online Tutoring Space

Creating your online tutoring space is like crafting the perfect holiday gift—thoughtful, personal, and a little bit magical! Start by selecting a cozy nook in your home where you can set up your virtual classroom. This could be a corner of your living room, a quiet bedroom, or even a spot in the kitchen. Make sure it's well-lit and free from distractions. A cheerful backdrop can add a festive touch, so consider hanging up some colorful holiday decorations or a fun educational poster. Remember, a warm and inviting atmosphere will put both you and your students in the holiday spirit!

Next, let's talk about the tech side of things. You don't need the fanciest gadgets to make your online tutoring space shine! A reliable computer or tablet, a good internet connection, and a webcam (or your device's built-in camera) are essential. Don't forget about audio! A simple pair of headphones with a microphone can help you communicate clearly with your students. Now is the perfect time to test everything out to avoid any tech hiccups during your first session. Think of it as your holiday tech pep rally—get everything warmed up and ready to go!

Once your space is set up, consider how you'll engage your students. Just like wrapping a gift, presentation matters!

Have a few fun tools at your disposal, such as interactive whiteboards or educational games that you can share on screen. You could even create some festive worksheets or activities themed around the holidays. This extra touch not only makes learning enjoyable but also helps you stand out as a tutor. Remember, it's not just about teaching; it's about creating memorable experiences that keep students excited to learn during their holiday break.

Now, let's sprinkle in some charm! Personalize your tutoring sessions by incorporating holiday themes into your lessons. For example, if you're tutoring math, why not use candy canes or holiday cookies as counting tools? If you're diving into reading, choose holiday stories that capture the spirit of the season. This approach keeps your students engaged and eager to learn. Plus, it can transform a regular tutoring session into a festive celebration, making it a win-win for everyone involved!

Finally, don't forget to market your new online tutoring services! Leverage social media to spread the word among friends, family, and local community groups. Share stories of your setup and the unique holiday-themed lessons you offer. You can even create special holiday packages or discounts to attract more students eager to make the most of their time off. With a little creativity and enthusiasm, your online tutoring space can become a beacon of learning and joy, helping families in need while you earn some extra cash for the holidays.

Attracting Students During the Holiday Season

The holiday season is a magical time, filled with twinkling lights and the sweet smell of freshly baked cookies. But for families looking to make extra money, it can also be a busy time of year filled with opportunities and creative ways to cash in. As kids find themselves with some free time during their holiday break, why not turn that time into a fun and profitable adventure? This is the perfect moment for families to come together, unleash their creativity, and explore the exciting world of holiday hustles.

First up, let's talk about seasonal crafts! Kids can tap into their artistic flair by creating handmade holiday decorations like ornaments, wreaths, and festive centerpieces. Set up a crafting station in your living room and gather supplies like glitter, ribbons, and paints. Once the masterpieces are complete, host a mini holiday fair right outside your home or set up an online shop on platforms like Etsy. Neighbors and friends will love the chance to purchase unique, handcrafted items that add a personal touch to their holiday celebrations.

Online tutoring is another fantastic way for older kids to earn some cash while helping others. As students take a break from school, many parents look for extra help in subjects like math, reading, or even holiday-themed crafts! If your child excels in a particular subject, they can set up virtual tutoring sessions. Not only will they earn money, but they'll also gain valuable teaching experience. Plus, it's a win-win when they can help younger kids master their schoolwork while pocketing some extra holiday dough.

For those who love to spread cheer through lights and decorations, Christmas light installation can be a fun side hustle. Kids can partner with parents to offer services to neighbors who may need some help brightening up their homes. With a little planning and safety in mind, they can climb up ladders, hang twinkling lights, and create stunning displays that will dazzle the neighborhood. Not only will they earn money, but they'll also get to enjoy the festive atmosphere while working together as a family.

Finally, the culinary arts can be a delightful way to bring in some extra holiday cash. Whether it's baking cookies, making holiday treats, or catering festive meals, the kitchen can be a bustling hub of creativity. Families can whip up batches of cookies or pies and sell them to neighbors or at local holiday events. Consider setting up a stand in your front yard or advertising via social media. With a sprinkle of holiday spirit and a dash of creativity, your family can turn those delicious treats into a sweet source of income, all while enjoying the flavors of the season together.

4

CHAPTER 4: LIGHTS, CAMERA, ACTION: CHRISTMAS LIGHT

Getting Started: Equipment and Safety

Ready to dive into the world of holiday hustles? First things first: you need to gather the right equipment! Depending on what hustle you choose—be it crafting, baking, or even outdoor decorating—a well-thought-out setup can make all the difference. For crafty families, consider gathering supplies like paints, brushes, fabrics, and any other materials you might need to create beautiful handmade decorations or gifts. If baking is your jam, stock up on baking trays, mixing bowls, and, of course, all those scrumptious ingredients. And for those planning to install Christmas lights or rent out equipment, make sure you have ladders, extension cords, and all the safety gear you can find. The better prepared you are, the more fun and successful your holiday hustle will be!

Now, let's talk safety! Holiday hustles can be a blast, but safety is the number one rule to keep the cheer alive. If you're climbing ladders to hang twinkling lights, make sure you have a buddy to hold the ladder steady. For those baking up a storm, always use oven mitts and be cautious with sharp utensils. Kids, be sure to ask an adult to help with tasks that require a bit more muscle or experience. Safety gear like goggles and gloves can also be your best friends, especially when working with tools or crafting supplies that might cause a mess. Remember, nothing kills the holiday spirit like an unexpected trip to the emergency room!

Once you have your equipment ready and your safety measures in place, it's time to set up your workspace. Whether it's a kitchen counter for baking or a cozy corner for crafting, make sure you have enough space to spread out and get creative. Keep your materials organized—nothing is more frustrating than hunting for that one elusive paintbrush! Make it festive! Add some holiday tunes, a cozy blanket, or even a little decoration to inspire your hustle. A cheerful environment can kick-start your creativity and make the hard work feel like a fun holiday project.

As you embark on your hustle, don't forget to budget for any additional equipment you might need along the way. If you're serious about your side gig, investing in quality tools can pay off in the long run. For instance, a sturdy set of baking pans can help you whip up delicious treats that will keep customers coming back for more. Or, if you're renting out holiday equipment, investing in good-quality decorations will ensure they look fabulous for your clients. Remember, the goal is to make some extra cash for the holidays, so think smart and shop wisely!

Finally, don't overlook the power of community and collaboration. Share your journey with friends and family, and don't hesitate to ask for advice or assistance. You might find a neighbor who can lend you a tool or someone willing to help you set up a booth at a holiday market. Plus, teaming up can make the experience a whole lot more enjoyable! Whether you're crafting with friends or baking together, the holiday spirit thrives in togetherness. So gather your loved ones, get those creative juices flowing, and let the hustling begin!

Pricing Your Installation Services

When it comes to pricing your installation services, think of it like decorating a holiday tree: a little sparkle here, a little shimmer there, and you've got a masterpiece! First, you want to cover your costs. If you're hanging those dazzling Christmas lights, consider the price of the lights, extension cords, and any tools you might need. Make a quick list of expenses and keep it handy. Remember, you want to make sure your hard work pays off, just like a perfectly wrapped gift under the tree!

Next up, let's sprinkle in some competitive magic. Take a peek at what other holiday hustlers in your area are charging for similar services. Are you the only elf in town offering Christmas light installation? That might just give you a little leeway to boost your prices! But if you notice a bunch of other elves competing for the same customers, you might want to keep your prices attractive. Think of it as a friendly competition to see who can create the most festive sparkle without breaking the bank.

Don't forget to add a dash of value! What unique twist do you bring to the table? Maybe you've got a knack for creating dazzling light displays that look like something out of a holiday movie. Perhaps you offer a package that includes a free consultation or a guarantee to come back and fix any bulbs that burn out. Highlight your special skills and services when setting your prices. Customers love knowing they're getting more than just a service; they want an experience that feels magical!

Now, let's talk about the sweet spot of pricing. You want to find that perfect balance where your customers feel they're getting a great deal while you're still making some jingle for yourself. A good rule of thumb is to consider your target hourly wage and how long you expect the job to take. If you think a project will take about three hours and you want to earn $15 an hour, then pricing your service at $45 is a great place to start. Keep in mind that the holiday season is all about giving and receiving, so flexibility can be key—don't be afraid to offer discounts for multiple jobs or referrals!

Lastly, be sure to communicate your pricing clearly. Create a festive flyer or post on social media that outlines your services and prices. Use cheerful language and holiday-themed visuals to catch the eye of potential customers. When people see your pricing upfront, they'll feel more comfortable reaching out for your jingle-worthy services. And remember, as you embark on this holiday hustle, the goal is not just to earn some extra cash but to spread joy and cheer throughout the community!

Promoting Your Light Installation Business

Promoting your light installation business can feel like decorating a giant Christmas tree—exciting, a bit overwhelming, and all about making the right connections. Start by tapping into your neighborhood. Nothing brings the holiday spirit quite like a dazzling display of lights, so hang up your own twinkling masterpieces and invite your neighbors to come take a look. You can even host a small open house, complete with hot cocoa and cookies, to showcase your work. Word of mouth is powerful, especially in tight-knit communities, and who knows? That neighbor who loves your setup might just want a similar sparkle in their own yard!

Social media is another shiny tool in your promotional toolbox. Create an Instagram account to showcase your installations, complete with before-and-after photos that make your work pop! Use fun hashtags like #LightUpTheHolidays and #TwinkleTime to reach a broader audience. Engage with your followers by asking them to share their own light displays or vote on their favorite designs. You could even run a contest where the winner receives a discount on their own light installation. This not only builds excitement but also creates a buzz about your business, making it easier for families to find and hire you.

Let's not forget the power of local community events. Join holiday fairs or festivals where you can set up a booth showcasing your services. Bring along an impressive portfolio of your past installations, and maybe even a few lights to create a mini display. Having a hands-on approach not only attracts attention but allows families to ask questions and get to know you better. You might even consider offering a special holiday promotion for those who book your services during the event. This way, you're not just selling a service; you're creating a memorable experience that families will associate with your brand.

Team up with other local businesses for cross-promotion. Perhaps a nearby bakery would love to partner with you to offer a holiday package: a festive light installation coupled with delicious gingerbread treats. Or, collaborate with a local florist to create a bundle that includes beautiful wreaths and lights to brighten up the front porch. These partnerships can amplify your reach, allowing you to tap into each other's customer bases and create a win-win situation for everyone involved.

Finally, don't underestimate the power of online platforms. Utilize local community groups on Facebook or Nextdoor to advertise your services. Share your story, how you got started, and the joy you find in lighting up homes for the holidays. Consider offering a discount for first-time customers or a referral bonus for those who spread the word about you. As the holiday season approaches, families will be looking for ways to make their homes festive, and your light installation business could be just what they need to create that magical atmosphere. Remember, each installation is not just about lights; it's about spreading joy and creating memories that families will cherish for years to come!

5

CHAPTER 5: WRAP IT UP: FREELANCE GIFT WRAPPING

Essentials for a Wrapping Station

Creating a wrapping station is a delightful way to turn a simple task into a fun experience while boosting your holiday hustle. First things first, choose a space that feels festive! Whether it's your kitchen table or a cozy corner of the living room, make sure it's well-lit and free of clutter. Add some holiday decorations to get everyone in the spirit—think twinkling lights, cheerful ornaments, or a favorite holiday mug filled with hot cocoa. The more festive the atmosphere, the more motivated you and your little helpers will be to wrap those gifts and earn some extra cash!

Next, gather all the essentials you'll need for your wrapping station. Stock up on colorful wrapping paper, tape, scissors, and gift tags. Don't forget a few fun extras, like ribbons, bows, and stickers to add some pizzazz to your packages. If you're feeling crafty, consider making your own wrapping paper from recycled materials, like brown paper bags or old newspaper! This not only saves money but also gives your gifts a unique touch that friends and family will love. Plus, it's a great way to involve the kids in a creative project that can lead to a little extra income.

Organization is key to a successful wrapping station. Set up a designated area for each supply to keep the space tidy and efficient. You might have one side for papers and another for tools. This not only helps you find what you need quickly but also makes it easier for kids to pitch in. As they learn how to wrap, they'll appreciate the importance of a tidy workspace, and you can turn this into a mini lesson about organization that can benefit them beyond the holidays. Who knew gift wrapping could double as a life skill?

Consider how you can leverage your wrapping station for some extra holiday cash. Offer your gift-wrapping services to friends, family, or neighbors who might be too busy to tackle it themselves. You could even set up a small booth at local holiday markets or community events. Don't forget to spread the word on social media—post pictures of your beautifully wrapped gifts and let people know you're available! This not only helps you make some money but also allows kids to learn about entrepreneurship in a fun way.

Lastly, don't forget to enjoy the process! Wrapping gifts is about more than just the final product; it's about creating memories together. Play your favorite holiday tunes, share stories about the gifts you're wrapping, and laugh at any wrapping mishaps that happen along the way. Celebrate your successes, no matter how small, and remember that each gift you wrap is another step toward making the holidays brighter for your family and your community. Embrace the joy of giving, and watch how your wrapping station becomes a hub of creativity and cheer!

Unique Wrapping Techniques to Wow Clients

When it comes to wrapping gifts, why settle for ordinary when you can create extraordinary? Unique wrapping techniques not only make your gifts stand out, but they can also become a fun side hustle during the holiday season. Imagine transforming a simple box into a work of art that brings smiles before the gift is even opened. With a few clever tricks up your sleeve, you can wow friends and family, and maybe even make a little extra cash while you're at it.

First up, why not try the art of fabric wrapping? Using fabric instead of traditional wrapping paper is not only eco-friendly but also adds a touch of elegance to your gifts. You can pick up some colorful fabric remnants at thrift stores or craft shops, and with a few simple knots and bows, you'll have a gift that's as beautiful as what's inside. Plus, you can promote your fabric-wrapping services to your friends and neighbors. Who wouldn't want a stunningly wrapped gift that's also reusable?

For those who love a bit of whimsy, consider using newspaper or old maps for a vintage-inspired look. Add some bright ribbons or twine, and you've got a conversation starter! This technique is not only budget-friendly but also gives a unique twist to your wrapping game. You can even create themed wrapping depending on the occasion—like using maps for a travel enthusiast. As you showcase your creativity, you can offer workshops for kids and families to join in on the fun of making their gifts look fabulous.

Don't forget about embellishments! A simple gift can be turned into a masterpiece with a few well-placed decorations. Think pinecones, dried citrus slices, or even handmade ornaments. These little touches show that you put thought and effort into each gift. You could even start offering a service where you help others make their gifts pop. How cool would it be to have a line of clients waiting for your festive flair?

Lastly, embrace the magic of upcycling! Collect items such as jars, boxes, or even old holiday cards and turn them into charming gift containers. Wrap a jar of homemade cookies with twine, or use a decorated box for small trinkets. Not only does this technique save money, but it also adds a personal touch that everyone will appreciate. Plus, you can share your upcycling journey online, inspiring others and potentially attracting clients who want you to wrap their gifts in style.

With these unique wrapping techniques, you'll not only impress your loved ones but also create opportunities to make some extra cash this holiday season. Get creative, have fun, and let your wrapping skills shine!

Finding Clients: Neighborhoods, Schools, and Online

When it comes to finding clients for your holiday hustle, think of your neighborhood as a treasure trove of opportunities. Start by walking around and checking out the festive spirit in the air. Knock on doors, or simply chat with your neighbors while taking a stroll. You might be surprised at how many families need a little extra help during the busy holiday season. Whether it's installing Christmas lights or finding someone to wrap gifts beautifully, your neighbors could be your first loyal customers. Plus, nothing beats the feeling of helping out those right next door while earning some extra cash!

Schools are buzzing with holiday cheer, making them an excellent place to connect with potential clients. Consider reaching out to parent-teacher associations or local school events. You could offer your services for events like holiday parties or craft fairs, where parents are often looking for unique gifts and treats. Set up a booth at a school fair to showcase your handmade decorations or baked goods. Not only will you tap into a ready-made audience of families, but you'll also create buzz and get the word out about your seasonal side hustle.

The online world is your playground when it comes to finding clients, so get ready to dive into the digital realm! Social media platforms like Facebook, Instagram, and even TikTok are perfect for showcasing your holiday talents. Create eye-catching posts or videos highlighting your gift-wrapping skills, holiday treats, or stunning decorations. Join local community groups online where families are searching for help during the holidays. You can offer your services, promote your crafts, or even share some festive tips to get people interested in what you have to offer.

Don't forget about the power of word-of-mouth! Encourage your friends and family to spread the word about your services. If you have a few happy clients, ask them for testimonials or referrals. You can even create a fun flyer or business card that you can distribute around your neighborhood or at local holiday events. Personal connections can make a world of difference, especially when people are looking for recommendations during the bustling holiday season.

Finally, remember to keep your services flexible and fun! Whether you're baking festive treats, wrapping gifts, or renting out holiday equipment, make sure to highlight the joy and creativity in what you do. Each interaction is an opportunity to spread cheer and connect with your clients. With a sprinkle of enthusiasm and a dash of creativity, you can turn your holiday hustle into a successful venture that not only brings in extra cash but also fills your heart with holiday spirit!

6

CHAPTER 6: BAKE IT TILL YOU MAKE IT

Holiday Treats That Sell Like Hotcakes Holiday treats can transform kitchens into bustling bakeries, and they're a sure-fire way to earn some extra cash during the festive season. With the scent of gingerbread and peppermint wafting through the air, families can turn their culinary creations into a sweet side hustle. From cookies to cakes, these holiday delights not only satisfy cravings but also bring in the bucks. So roll up your sleeves, grab your mixing bowls, and let's whip up some holiday treats that will have everyone lining up like it's Black Friday!

First on the list are classic cookies. Who can resist a tray of warm, gooey chocolate chip cookies? Or perhaps festive sugar cookies decorated with colorful icing? These treats are easy to make in large batches, and they sell like hotcakes at local holiday markets or even through social media. Kids can get creative by offering themed cookie decorating kits that families can enjoy together. It's not just about the cookies; it's about creating memories that bring smiles and, of course, some extra cash into the household!

Next up, we have decadent cupcakes and cakes. With a little creativity, you can transform ordinary cupcakes into holiday masterpieces topped with candy canes, sprinkles, or even mini ornaments. Consider offering a variety of flavors, from classic vanilla to rich red velvet. A well-decorated cake can be the centerpiece of any holiday gathering, so why not take pre-orders for those special occasions? Families will appreciate the convenience, and you'll be raking in the dough while spreading holiday cheer!

Don't forget about the magic of home-made candy and treats! Fudge, truffles, and caramel popcorn are just a few sweet ideas that can fly off the shelves. Set up a candy-making station at home, and get the kids involved—it's a fun way to bond and learn about entrepreneurship. Packaging them in festive boxes or jars can make your treats even more appealing. Remember, presentation is key! A little creativity can turn simple sweets into desirable gifts that people will be eager to buy.

Finally, consider offering seasonal baking classes or workshops for families looking to hone their baking skills. This could be a fun way for kids to earn money while sharing their love of baking with others. You could even host online sessions, making it accessible for everyone. Whether it's teaching how to make the perfect pie crust or decorating holiday cookies, these classes can be a delightful way to engage with the community and make some extra cash while spreading holiday joy. So gather your ingredients and get ready to start a holiday hustle that will make your family's season bright!

Setting Up Your Home Bakery Legally

Setting up your home bakery legally is like icing on the cake - it may seem tricky at first, but once you get the hang of it, it's a piece of cake! Before you whip up those delicious treats and share them with the world, you need to sprinkle in some legal magic to ensure everything is sweet and above board. The first step is to check your local laws and regulations.

Each state has different rules regarding home-based businesses, especially when it comes to food. A little research goes a long way, so grab your favorite holiday cookie and start browsing your local health department's website to find out what permits or licenses you may need.

Next up, let's talk about the kitchen! Your home sweet home needs to be a safe zone for baking. This means ensuring that your kitchen meets health and safety standards. You might need to make some adjustments, like keeping your workspace clean and organized, and possibly even investing in some basic food safety training. Think of it as a fun holiday project! You can involve the kids in sprucing up the kitchen and making it a cozy baking haven. Plus, by teaching them about cleanliness in the kitchen, you're not only making it festive but also giving them valuable life skills!

Now, let's get to the fun part – creating a business plan that sparkles! Outline your baking specialties, pricing, and how you plan to market your treats. Will you focus on holiday-themed goodies, or maybe some classic family recipes? Consider how you'll reach your customers. Social media is a fabulous way to spread the word about your delicious offerings. You can post mouthwatering photos of your creations, set up an Instagram account, or even make a fun TikTok video showing your baking process. Remember, the more creative and engaging, the better!

After setting up your plan, it's time to get your paperwork in order. Depending on where you live, you might need to apply for a business license, food handler's permit, or even register your bakery name. Don't let this step scare you; it's just a little paperwork to ensure you're ready to bake safely and legally. You can even turn it into a family activity! Everyone can pitch in by filling out forms together or brainstorming names for your bakery that reflect your holiday spirit.

Finally, consider getting the word out through local events and markets. Many communities host holiday fairs where you can showcase your baked goodies. This not only helps you meet potential customers but also builds a sense of community. Plus, nothing beats the joy of seeing someone's face light up when they take a bite of your delicious creation! With the right legal setup, a dash of creativity, and a sprinkle of community spirit, your home bakery can be the sweetest holiday hustle for you and your family!

Marketing Your Baked Goods for Holiday Parties

When the holiday season rolls around, the scent of freshly baked cookies and warm pies wafts through the air, creating a festive atmosphere that's hard to resist. This is the perfect time for families looking to make some extra cash to tap into the joy of baking! Whether you're whipping up batches of your famous gingerbread men or crafting decadent chocolate cakes, marketing your baked goods for holiday parties can turn your love for baking into a delightful money-making adventure. So, let's sprinkle some creativity and fun into your baking hustle!

First things first, let's talk about presentation. Your baked goods need to look as scrumptious as they taste! Get crafty with your packaging—think festive boxes tied with colorful ribbons or clear bags adorned with holiday stickers. You could even add a personal touch by including a handwritten recipe card. When people see your beautifully packaged treats, they'll be tempted to buy them for their holiday gatherings. Don't forget to snap some mouth-watering photos of your creations to share on social media. A well-taken pic can be the difference between a sale and a missed opportunity!

Next, let your friends and family be your first taste testers and biggest promoters. Word-of-mouth is a powerful marketing tool, especially when it comes to food! Host a little tasting party and invite your neighbors, family, and friends to try your baked goods. Encourage them to spread the word and share your social media posts. You can also create a fun referral program—if someone refers a new customer to you, they get a discount on their next order. This not only encourages sales but creates a sense of community around your baking business.

As the holidays approach, tap into local events and gatherings. Farmers' markets, craft fairs, and school holiday parties are perfect opportunities to showcase your baked goods. Set up a cheerful booth filled with your treats, and make sure to engage with customers. A warm smile and a friendly chat can go a long way! You can even offer samples to entice passersby. If you can't set up a booth, consider partnering with local businesses to sell your goodies. They will appreciate the unique offerings, and you'll gain exposure to their customers!

Finally, don't forget about online marketing. Social media platforms are bustling with holiday cheer and people looking for festive treats. Create enticing posts about your baked goods, share behind-the-scenes videos of your baking process, and engage with your followers. Consider setting up an online ordering system through platforms like Facebook or Instagram. You could even create themed holiday packages, like "Holiday Cookie Samplers" or "Festive Dessert Platters," to make ordering easy and fun for your customers. With a sprinkle of creativity and a dash of determination, your baking side hustle can turn into a merry little business this holiday season!

7

CHAPTER 7: HANDMADE HOLIDAY CHEER

Crafting Unique Decorations that Sell

Crafting unique decorations that sell is like turning your creativity into cash, and what better time to do it than during the holiday season? Picture this: your home is filled with the scents of pine and cinnamon, and you're surrounded by kids excited to create something magical. The best part? Those creations could soon be flying off the shelves! Whether it's charming ornaments, glittery wreaths, or whimsical garlands, each piece you make can tell a story and spark joy in someone's home while fattening your wallet.

Start by gathering materials that are not only affordable but also easy to work with. Think about items you might already have lying around the house—old holiday cards, fabric scraps, or even pine cones from your backyard. These treasures can be transformed into stunning decorations with just a little imagination and some crafty hands. Encourage the kids to brainstorm ideas and let their creativity run wild. The more unique and fun the decorations are, the more likely they'll catch the eye of potential buyers.

Next, consider showcasing your crafts in a way that tells a story. Set up a festive display in your front yard or at local holiday markets. Add lights, music, and even a hot cocoa stand to create a magical atmosphere that draws in customers. If you decide to sell online, take great photos of your creations. Natural light and a clean background can make your decorations pop, and don't forget to write catchy descriptions that highlight what makes each item special. Remember, people love a good backstory, especially during the holidays!

Pricing your handmade decorations can feel tricky, but don't stress! Start by calculating the cost of materials and your time. Keep in mind that uniqueness can command a higher price, especially if you're creating items that are hard to find elsewhere. You might even consider offering custom options—like personalized ornaments that let buyers add names or special dates. This not only increases the value of your product but also makes it more meaningful for those looking to give gifts from the heart.

Lastly, don't underestimate the power of social media to spread the word about your creations. Share photos of your process, the finished products, and even happy customers enjoying your decorations. Encourage family and friends to share your posts, creating a ripple effect that could lead to more sales. And remember, this is not just about making money; it's about building memories and sharing the joy of the season with others. So grab those glitter, gather the kiddos, and get crafting—your holiday hustle awaits!

Pricing Your Handmade Goods

Pricing your handmade goods can feel like trying to solve a puzzle without all the pieces. You don't want to make your creations so pricey that they scare off potential buyers, but you also don't want to give them away for a song. The key lies in striking that perfect balance. Begin by assessing the cost of materials and labor. Write down every little thing you spent on your project, from glitter and glue to the time you spent crafting while sipping hot cocoa. This gives you a solid foundation to understand the minimum price you need to charge to keep your holiday hustle afloat.

Next, think about your audience. Families looking to make their holidays special might appreciate the unique charm of your handmade goods, but they also have budgets to consider. Take a stroll through local craft fairs or browse online marketplaces to see what similar items are selling for. This research will help you gauge the competition and price your items competitively while still valuing your hard work. Remember, you're not just selling a product; you're offering a piece of your creativity and joy!

Once you have a baseline price, it's time to sprinkle in some extra magic. Consider the value of your unique selling proposition—what makes your goods stand out? Perhaps your ornaments are made from recycled materials, or your wreaths come with a handmade bow.

Highlighting these special features can allow you to justify a slightly higher price. After all, buyers love stories, and if your product has a tale that tugs at heartstrings, they may be more willing to part with their cash.

Don't forget about the importance of seasonal pricing strategies. As the holidays approach, people are often willing to spend a little more for something that feels festive and fun. You can create special holiday bundles or themed sets that add value without breaking the bank for your customers. Think about offering a discount for bulk purchases—like a "buy two, get one free" deal. This not only encourages sales but also brings joy to families looking to decorate their homes or gift something special.

Finally, keep an eye on your sales and be ready to adjust your prices as needed. If your items are flying off the shelves, you might be underpricing your goods. On the flip side, if they're sitting around collecting dust, it might be time to re-think your strategy. Pricing isn't a one-and-done deal; it's an evolving process. So embrace the journey and let your creativity shine, because your handmade goods have the potential to bring joy to many families during the holiday season.

Selling Online vs. Local Craft Fairs

When it comes to making a few extra bucks during the holiday season, families have two exciting avenues to explore: selling online and showcasing your crafts at local craft fairs. Each option has its own charm, just like hot cocoa with marshmallows versus a cozy cup of apple cider. Selling online offers the convenience of reaching a broader audience right from your living room, while local craft fairs provide the thrill of face-to-face interactions with eager shoppers. Let's dive into the jolly pros and cons of each to help you decide where to set up your holiday hustle!

Selling online is like opening the door to a world of possibilities. With platforms like Etsy, eBay, and social media market-places, you can showcase your handmade decorations, baked goodies, or even rental items for the holidays. Plus, you can operate in your pajamas while sipping that delicious hot cocoa! Online selling allows you to reach customers beyond your local community. However, it does come with its own set of challenges, such as managing shipping, ensuring product visibility, and navigating the digital marketplace. But don't worry, with a sprinkle of creativity and a dash of marketing savvy, you can turn your online store into a festive wonderland!

On the other hand, local craft fairs are like a holiday party where everyone's invited! Setting up a booth at a fair allows you to connect directly with customers, sharing your story and passion. Picture this: your handmade ornaments glistening in the warm glow of holiday lights as families stroll by, excited to find the perfect gift. Plus, the festive atmosphere, complete with cheerful music and delicious snacks, can make the whole experience feel like a celebration. While local fairs may have limited reach, the personal connections and immediate feedback can be priceless, especially for kids looking to learn the ropes of entrepreneurship.

However, before you dive into either option, consider the time and effort involved. Selling online often requires you to invest time in taking high-quality photos, writing catchy descriptions, and handling orders. Meanwhile, local craft fairs typically involve setting up your booth, managing your inventory, and engaging with customers. If your family is all hands on deck, it could turn into a fun bonding experience. But if you're juggling other responsibilities, one option may suit your family's schedule better than the other.

In the end, whether you choose to sell online or at local craft fairs, the key to success lies in your enthusiasm and cre-ativity. Encourage your kids to brain-storm ideas, create unique products, and even design their booth displays. This holiday season, let the spirit of entrepre-neurship shine bright in your family as you explore the joy of making extra money together. With a little planning and a lot of holiday cheer, you're bound to turn your hustle into a delightful ad-venture that warms both hearts and wal-lets!

8

CHAPTER 8: RENT-A-FESTIVITY

What to Rent: Equipment Ideas for Families

When the holiday season rolls around, families often seek creative ways to bring in extra cash without breaking the bank. One fantastic idea is to rent out equipment that can make holiday celebrations even more special. Think of all the fun items families use during the holidays: inflatables, lights, tables, and chairs for gatherings, and even catering equipment for those big dinners. By tapping into these needs, your family can turn a profit while providing a service that makes the holiday spirit shine even brighter.

Start by considering what you already own that can be rented out. Do you have a dazzling light display that could turn any yard into a winter wonderland? Or perhaps a set of folding tables and chairs perfect for those festive feasts? You might even own an inflatable Santa or a reindeer that could bring joy to your neighbors. Each of these items can be a valuable asset, particularly during the holiday season when everyone is looking to create a festive atmosphere without spending a fortune.

Next, broaden your horizons to include equipment that could be useful for holiday projects. Renting out baking supplies like mixers or catering equipment can attract families looking to whip up their favorite holiday treats. You could also consider renting tools for DIY holiday decorations. This way, families can craft their unique ornaments or centerpieces while you earn a little extra jingle for your efforts. Don't forget about renting out tech gadgets as well; think projectors for holiday movie nights or speakers for festive gatherings.

Marketing your rental business can be fun and engaging. Create eye-catching flyers or social media posts showcasing your available items, emphasizing how they can enhance the holiday experience. Collaborate with local schools or community centers to spread the word, or host a holiday open house where families can come see your equipment in action. Word of mouth is powerful, especially when it comes to community connections during the holidays.

Lastly, make sure to set clear rental prices and terms to ensure a smooth process for both you and your clients. Consider offering package deals for multiple items or discounts for early book-ings. This not only makes your offerings more attractive but also encourages fam-ilies to plan ahead for their festive gath-erings. With a little creativity and community spirit, renting out holiday equipment can become a successful side hustle for your family, allowing you to spread joy while filling your pockets with extra holiday cheer.

Creating a Rental Business Plan

Creating a rental business plan is like drawing up a treasure map for your holi-day hustle. It's exciting to think about all the ways you can make extra cash during the festive season, and renting out items can be a fantastic way to do just that! Imagine turning your unused holiday decorations or equipment into a money-making machine. The first step in your plan is to take stock of what you have. Do you have extra Christmas lights, in-flatable decorations, or even tables and chairs for holiday parties gathering dust in your garage? Jot down everything you think others might want to rent for their celebrations. This is your inventory, and it's the start of your merry money-making adventure!

Next, you'll want to think about how you'll get the word out. In this digital age, social media is your best friend! Create fun, colorful posts showcasing your rental items. Use bright pictures of your twinkling lights and cheerful decorations to grab attention. Don't forget to sprinkle in some holiday cheer by sharing festive tips or DIY decoration ideas. You can even ask friends and family to spread the word. The more people know about your rental business, the more interest you'll generate, and soon enough, you'll have a line of holiday party planners ready to rent from you!

Setting your prices is the next important step, and it's like finding the perfect balance on a seesaw. You want to make sure you're charging enough to cover your costs and earn some jingle, but not so much that customers will look elsewhere. Research what similar items are renting for in your area and set competitive prices. Offering special deals for longer rentals or package deals can also entice customers. For example, if someone rents your lights, offer a discount on other items like lawn decorations. Everyone loves a good deal, especially during the holiday rush!

Once you've got your inventory, marketing, and pricing sorted, it's time to think about the logistics. Create a simple system for managing your rentals. How will people reserve items? Will you require a deposit? Make sure to outline clear pick-up and drop-off times. You could even create a fun rental agreement that feels festive! Keep track of who rented what and when, so you can ensure everything is returned in tip-top shape. Being organized will not only make your life easier but will also impress your customers, leading to repeat business and referrals.

Finally, let's talk about the magic of customer service. Being friendly and responsive can turn a one-time renter into a loyal fan. Make sure you're available to answer questions and provide assistance. If someone has a problem with your rental, be quick to resolve it with a smile. Consider adding personal touches, like a thank-you note with a small holiday treat when they return their items. These little gestures create joy and encourage customers to come back for more. With your rental business plan in hand, you'll be ready to spread holiday cheer and cash in on the festive fun!

Finding Your Target Market

Finding your target market is like embarking on a treasure hunt, and the rewards can be bountiful. For families looking to hustle through the holiday season, it's essential to know who might be interested in your jingle-worthy offerings. Start by thinking about the needs and desires of your community. Are there busy parents who might be overwhelmed with the holiday chaos? Perhaps there are neighbors who love to decorate but need a little help. By identifying these groups, you can tailor your services to fit perfectly into their holiday plans, making your offerings irresistible.

Next, consider the power of social media. Platforms like Facebook, Instagram, and TikTok are not just for scrolling; they're vibrant marketplaces bustling with potential customers. Create eye-catching posts showcasing your seasonal crafts, mouth-watering holiday treats, or even videos of your dazzling Christmas light installations. By tagging local groups and using relevant hashtags, you can reach families in your area who are searching for unique ways to celebrate without the stress. Remember, a little creativity goes a long way in capturing attention and spreading the word about your holiday hustles.

Don't underestimate the power of word-of-mouth! Tell your friends, family, and neighbors about your holiday side hustles. They can be your biggest cheerleaders and help spread the news. Consider hosting a small showcase event at home where you demonstrate your skills—whether it's gift wrapping, baking, or crafting. This not only gives potential customers a taste of what you offer but also builds a sense of community around your ventures. The more personal your approach, the more likely your neighbors will trust you and want to support your holiday hustle.

Think about local events or fairs during the holiday season. These gatherings are fantastic opportunities to get your products and services in front of potential customers. Set up a booth to sell your handmade holiday decorations or offer samples of your baked goods. Get creative with your presentation; a little festive flair can attract the attention of families looking for that special something to make their holiday celebrations brighter. Plus, it's a fun way to connect face-to-face and create lasting relationships with customers who may return year after year.

Lastly, don't forget the online marketplace! Websites like Etsy and local selling groups can be gold mines for seasonal crafts and decorations. List your services for online tutoring, gift wrapping, or even catering, and watch as families in need of these services flock to you. Make sure to include engaging descriptions and appealing photos to showcase your unique talents. With a bit of effort and creativity, you'll discover that finding your target market is not just about the hustle—it's about building connections that make the holiday season a little brighter for everyone involved.

9

CHAPTER 9: GET THE KIDS INVOLVED: FAMILY-FRIENDLY

Ideas for Kids to Earn Money

Kids today have a treasure trove of opportunities to earn some extra cash, especially during the holiday season. Whether you're looking to boost your pocket money for that must-have toy or save up for something special, there are plenty of fun and creative ways to do just that. The holidays are a magical time, and with a sprinkle of enthusiasm and a dash of creativity, kids can turn their ideas into a money-making adventure. So, let's dive into some exciting ideas that can help young entrepreneurs shine bright this festive season!

First up, let's talk about seasonal crafts. Kids can unleash their inner artist by creating holiday-themed crafts and selling them online or at local markets. Think handmade ornaments, festive cards, or even adorable decorations for the home. With a little guidance from parents, children can set up a small shop on social media or join a local craft fair, turning their creativity into cash! Plus, there's nothing quite like the joy of seeing others appreciate your hard work and artistic flair.

For those who excel in school, online tutoring can be a fantastic way to earn money while helping others. With holiday break approaching, many students look for extra help to catch up or get ahead. Kids can offer their expertise in subjects they excel in, creating a fun and interactive learning experience. Imagine turning your knowledge into a holiday hustle while making new friends and boosting someone's confidence—all from the comfort of home!

Now, let's brighten things up with Christmas light installation! Many families love to deck their halls for the holidays but might not have the time or energy to hang those twinkling lights. Kids can team up with a parent to offer their services as a festive decorating duo. It's a win-win: they get to enjoy the holiday spirit while earning some jingle in their pockets! With a little creativity in design and a keen eye for detail, kids can make homes sparkle and shine, spreading joy throughout the neighborhood.

Baking and catering can also be a delectable way for kids to earn some extra dough. With holiday treats like cookies, cakes, and festive snacks being in high demand, young bakers can whip up delicious goodies to sell to family and friends. Setting up a holiday bake sale can be an exciting project that not only helps kids learn about entrepreneurship but also brings smiles to people's faces as they indulge in sweet delights. Whether it's a simple cookie platter or a grand holiday cake, every baked good can bring in some sweet profits!

Finally, let's not forget about the potential of renting out holiday equipment and decorations. Many families love to celebrate with festive items, but purchasing everything can be pricey. Kids can offer rental services for holiday decorations, lights, or even inflatable yard displays. By collaborating with parents, they can create a fun rental business that caters to their community's needs. This idea not only helps families save money but also allows kids to learn about responsibility and customer service while having a blast!

With these ideas in hand, kids can embark on their holiday hustles, turning their creativity and skills into cash. Each endeavor not only provides a chance to earn money but also offers valuable life lessons in entrepreneurship, teamwork, and the joy of giving back to the community. So, grab those holiday hats and get ready to jingle all the way to the bank!

Teaching Kids About Money Management

Teaching kids about money management can be one of the most rewarding gifts you can give them, especially during the holiday hustle. The festive season is not just about receiving gifts but also about understanding the value of money and how to make it work for them. Start by introducing the concept of saving and spending wisely. Encourage your little ones to set aside a portion of any money they earn from their holiday side hustles, like selling handmade decorations or offering to help with Christmas light installation. They'll soon discover that saving a little can lead to big rewards!

Next up, let's talk about budgeting! Kids love the idea of having their own money, but they need to learn how to use it wisely. Create a simple budget together for their holiday earnings. Whether they're wrapping gifts for neighbors or baking cookies for a school bake sale, help them categorize their income and expenses. You can even make it a fun game by using colorful charts or stickers to track their progress. This will not only teach them the importance of budgeting but also make them feel like real money managers.

Now, sprinkle in some lessons about earning money. Highlight all the exciting ways they can hustle during the holiday season. From online tutoring for peers who need help with their homework to renting out holiday decorations, the opportunities are endless. Make a list together and encourage them to think creatively about what they can offer. If they love baking, remind them that a plate of festive cookies can turn into a sweet little profit! The key is to keep the mood light and fun while instilling a sense of entrepreneurship.

As they dive into their activities, it's important to discuss the idea of reinvestment. Teach them that sometimes, spending a little to make a lot is a smart move. For instance, if they earn money from selling crafts, they might consider using a portion of those earnings to buy better supplies or tools for their next project. This not only enhances their skills but also helps them understand the concept of investment in business. Encourage them to think of their side hustles as a mini-business, where every decision can lead to greater success.

Finally, wrap up your money management lessons with the importance of giving back. The holiday season is all about kindness and generosity, and what better way to teach this than by encouraging them to donate a small portion of their earnings to a charity or a family in need? This will help them appreciate the value of money beyond their own needs and desires. Not only will they learn money management skills, but they'll also cultivate empathy and a spirit of giving. By blending practical skills with playful activities, you'll set the stage for your kids to become savvy money managers while enjoying the magic of the holiday season.

Fun Family Projects to Boost Holiday Spirit

Gather the family around for some festive fun with projects that not only spread holiday cheer but also help you boost your holiday budget! Start by diving into seasonal craft selling. Gather supplies like paper, glitter, and paint, and let your creativity flow. You can create handmade ornaments, holiday cards, or even unique decorations that can be sold online or at local craft fairs. This project not only ignites your holiday spirit but also teaches kids the value of crafting and entrepreneurship. Plus, who doesn't love a homemade gift?

Next up, why not turn your home into a holiday wonderland with Christmas light installation? Get the kids involved in planning the layout and design. This can be an exciting way to bond while also showing off your festive flair to the neighborhood. You can even offer to help friends and family with their decorations for a small fee. Not only will you be spreading joy with your twinkling lights, but you'll also be creating a little extra cash flow for those holiday expenses.

Freelance gift wrapping is another delightful way to make some holiday cash! Set up a wrapping station at home with all sorts of colorful papers, ribbons, and embellishments. Encourage the kids to help wrap gifts for family and friends, and consider offering your services to others in the community. You could even create a fun social media post showcasing your wrapping skills, enticing people to hire you for the best-wrapped gifts in town!

If baking is more your family's style, turn your kitchen into a holiday bakery. Whip up batches of cookies, cakes, or festive treats, and then sell them in your neighborhood or at local markets. Kids can help with measuring, mixing, and decorating. This sweet side hustle not only fills your home with delicious aromas but also creates opportunities for family bonding and learning how to handle a small business. Plus, who can resist homemade goodies during the holidays?

Lastly, consider renting out holiday equipment and decor. After all, many families want to celebrate but might not have all the necessary items. Gather up any extra lights, decorations, or even holiday-themed items you own, and offer them for rent. Kids can help with inventory and marketing, making it a fun project that teaches them about resourcefulness and community spirit. These family projects not only bring joy and creativity into your home but also help you earn a little extra cash to make this holiday season extra special.

10

CHAPTER 10: THE JOY OF GIVING

Creating Family Traditions Around Your Hustles

Creating family traditions around your hustles can be a delightful way to bond and create lasting memories while also bringing in some extra cash during the holiday season. Think of these traditions as your family's unique holiday recipe, blending together fun, creativity, and the spirit of giving. Whether it's setting up a cozy craft corner or gathering around the kitchen, each tradition can be as special as the holiday itself. So, gather your crew, roll up your sleeves, and let's get crafting some family traditions that will not only bring joy but also jingle in some extra cash!

Start by choosing a signature hustle that resonates with everyone in the family. Perhaps you can dive into seasonal craft selling together, where each family member contributes a unique item. Kids can create handmade ornaments, while adults can whip up decorative wreaths or festive centerpieces. Set aside a weekend as your family craft day, complete with hot cocoa, holiday music, and plenty of glitter. This not only sets the stage for creativity but also turns hard work into a fun-filled day. At the end of it, you'll have a treasure trove of goodies ready to sell, and memories that sparkle brighter than the decorations.

Another fantastic idea is to turn baking into a family tradition. Gather the family in the kitchen to whip up holiday treats destined for your freelance baking and catering hustle. Each family member can choose their favorite recipe, from gingerbread cookies to peppermint bark. Make it a competition to see who can come up with the most creative treat to sell at local holiday markets. As you bake together, share stories and laughter, turning the kitchen into a festive hub. Not only will you create delicious goodies, but you'll also build a sense of teamwork and togetherness that's sweeter than any frosting.

Consider the joy of family-led holiday decorating as a tradition, especially if you decide to rent out holiday equipment and décor. Set aside a day for the family to transform your home into a winter wonderland. Involve everyone in choosing decorations and setting up lights. Make it a fun challenge to see who can come up with the most dazzling display. Capture the moments with photos, and don't forget to involve the kids in planning how this beautiful setup can be rented out. This not only fosters creativity but also teaches the kids about entrepreneurship in a playful manner.

Lastly, establish a family tradition of giving back. As you hustle and earn during the holidays, set aside a portion of your earnings for a charitable cause. Take the kids along to deliver toys, meals, or donations to those in need. This wonderful tradition not only helps teach the importance of generosity but also reinforces the idea that your hustles are not just about making money; they're about making a difference. By combining your entrepreneurial spirit with a heart for giving, you create a legacy that will inspire your children for years to come.

Planning for Self-Care During the Busy Season

Planning for self-care during the busy season is just as important as planning your holiday hustle. As families dive into making extra money through various festive endeavors, it's crucial to carve out time for self-care amidst the hustle and bustle. This holiday season, don't forget to sprinkle some joy and relaxation into your calendar, so you can tackle your side gigs with a smile instead of a frown. After all, a jolly spirit makes for a more successful holiday season!

First things first, set aside specific time for yourself on your busy calendar. Whether it's a cozy evening with hot cocoa and a favorite holiday movie, or a brisk walk in the winter wonderland, these little moments of joy will recharge your batteries. Consider scheduling a weekly self-care night where you can indulge in some pampering. Light some candles, put on your favorite tunes, and treat yourself to a bubble bath or a DIY spa session at home. You'll be amazed at how much more energy and positivity you'll bring to your holiday hustles when you take care of yourself.

Next, don't forget to involve the whole family in your self-care plans. Create a family tradition that celebrates both the festive spirit and relaxation. Perhaps a weekly family game night or a baking session where you all whip up some delicious treats together. These moments not only strengthen family bonds but also provide a much-needed break from the rush of holiday preparations. Plus, it's a great way to enjoy the fruits of your side hustle baking and catering while keeping the holiday spirit alive!

Another playful way to incorporate self-care is to engage in some light-hearted activities that foster creativity and relaxation. How about a family craft night where everyone can create hand-made holiday decorations? This is not only a fun way to unwind but could also inspire your own seasonal craft selling venture! Set up a crafting station with supplies, put on some festive music, and let the creativity flow. You'll end up with beautiful decorations for your home while also exploring new ideas for your side hustle.

Lastly, remember the importance of rest. During the busy holiday season, it can feel tempting to burn the midnight oil, but sleep is essential for keeping your energy levels high. Prioritize those cozy nights where you tuck into bed early, allowing your body to recover from the day's hustle. When you feel well-rested, you'll be more productive and enthusiastic about your side gigs, whether it's wrapping gifts or installing Christmas lights. So, as you plan your holiday hustles, don't forget to plan for self-care—it's the secret ingredient for a successful and joyful holiday season!

Giving Back: Using Your Hustle to Help Others

In the spirit of the season, let's talk about how your hustle can sprinkle a little extra joy into the lives of others. It's not just about making some cash for that shiny new toy or the perfect holiday gift; it's also about giving back to the community that supports us. Imagine transforming your holiday hustle into a beacon of hope for families facing tough times. Whether it's helping out at a local charity, donating a portion of your earnings, or using your skills to uplift others, you have the power to spread kindness and cheer.

First up, let's discuss how seasonal craft selling can be a win-win for you and your community. Picture this: you create beautiful handmade ornaments or festive decorations, and for every item sold, you donate a portion to a local food bank or shelter. Not only are you making extra money, but you're also sharing the joy of the holidays with those who need it most. Plus, crafting is a fantastic way to bond with your kids; get them involved in making items that can brighten someone's day. Talk about a holiday tradition that warms the heart!

Now, if you're gearing up for holiday break, online tutoring could be your ticket to not only earning some extra bucks but also making a meaningful impact. Many families struggle with keeping their kids engaged while school is out, so why not offer your tutoring services? You can help students with their studies while donating a part of your earnings to a local charity or school initiative. It's a beautiful cycle of learning and giving that can turn your expertise into a source of joy for both you and your community.

Have you ever thought about turning your knack for Christmas light installation into a charitable endeavor? You can offer your services to neighbors and donate a portion of your fees to community causes. Everyone loves a dazzling display of lights during the holidays, and your skills can light up the night while also lighting up the lives of those in need. Plus, it's an excellent way to spread holiday cheer as you help neighbors deck their halls with style!

Lastly, if you're a whiz in the kitchen, side hustle baking and catering can not only fill your pockets but also fill stomachs in your community. Bake those scrumptious cookies and cakes, but why stop there? You can host a bake sale where all the proceeds go to support local charities or families in need. It's a delightful way to share your culinary creations while making a positive impact. As you gather your family for holiday baking, remember that your hustle can be the gift that keeps on giving, spreading warmth and love one cookie at a time.